from **So We'll Go No More a Roving**
Lord Byron (1788-1824)

So, we'll go no more a roving
So late into the night,
Though the heart be still as loving,
And the moon be still as bright.

…

Though the night was made for loving,
And the day returns too soon,
Yet we'll go no more a roving
By the light of the moon.

At Home

A collection of poems

LAUTUS PRESS

Also published by Lautus Press

Washing Lines: A collection of poems
Strings of Pearls: A collection of poems
Shorelines: A collection of poems
Treelines: A collection of poems
all selected by Janie Hextall and Barbara McNaught

This collection was first published in 2023
Lautus Press, Ryton House, Lechlade, GL7 3AR
www.lautuspress.co.uk

ISBN: 978-0-9568265-4-1

© Janie Hextall and Barbara McNaught 2023

Designed and typeset in Minion Pro and P22 Underground
by Neil Morgan Design, Cheltenham
Printed by Holywell Press, Oxford

A CIP catalogue record for this book is available from the British Library

Contents

Lord Byron *So We'll Go No More a Roving*	Frontispiece
Seamus Heaney *Scaffolding*	8
Eavan Boland *A Ballad of Home*	9
Charles Tomlinson *The Door*	10
Esther Morgan *The first warm morning*	11
Imtiaz Dharker *This Room*	12
Esme *Home*	13
Robert Hull *Table*	14
Katherine Mansfield *Camomile Tea*	16
Gwen Harwood *Cups*	17
Jeanne Marie Beaumont *When I Am in the Kitchen*	18
Jane Clarke *Daily Bread*	19
Nina Bogin *Wooden Spoons*	20
Dennis O'Driscoll *Home*	21
Hugo Williams *Dinner with my Mother*	22
Ted Kooser *Zenith*	24
D H Lawrence *Piano*	25
Clive Wilmer *The Kitchen Table*	26
Penelope Shuttle *In the Kitchen*	28
Ted Kooser *A Winter Morning*	29
Cynthia Fuller *Guests*	30
Yves Bonnefoy *Let a Place be Made*	31
Beverley Bie Brahic *Teapot*	32
Jehane Markham *The Sofa*	34
Seamus Heaney *A Sofa in the Forties*	35
D A Prince *Hearth*	36
Jackie Kay *Winter Heart*	37
Michael Longley *An Amish Rug*	38
Carol Ann Duffy *Anne Hathaway*	39
Edna St Vincent Millay *Figs and Thistles: First Fig*	40
Katherine Mansfield *The Candle*	41
Deryn Rees-Jones *Sky Canoe*	42
Anon *Bed*	43

Edgar Guest *Midnight in the Pantry*	44
D A Prince *Spice Jars*	45
William Carlos Williams *This Is Just to Say*	46
Beverley Bie Brahic *Tango*	47
David Scott *The Slicing of Carrots*	48
Esther Morgan *This Morning*	49
Maya Angelou *Woman Work*	50
Joyce Sutphen *Canning*	51
Anon *Polly Put the Kettle On*	52
Dorothy Aldis *Setting the Table*	53
Edip Cansever *Table*	54
Rosemerry Wahtola Trommer *Setting*	55
Osip Mandelstam *Night Piece*	56
Ted Hughes *Wind*	57
Wendy Cope *Being Boring*	58
Ruby Archer *A Rainy Sunday*	59
Hugo Williams *Desk Duty*	60
Catherine Flynn *Instructions for a Bookcase*	62
John Fuller *The Chair*	63
Margaret Atwood *Year of the Hen*	64
Mahendra Solanki *Home*	66
Oswald Mbuyiseni Mtshali *Inside my Zulu Hut*	67
Edward Thomas *Home*	68
Jim Carruth *Homecoming*	69
Li T'ai-po *Autumn River Song*	70
Amy Lowell *The Fruit Garden Path*	71
Carol Ann Duffy *Prayer*	72
Peter Didsbury *An Expedition*	73
Olav H Hauge *Leaf-huts and Snow-houses*	74
Grace Wells *Lattice*	75
Pablo Neruda *Sonnet XXXIII*	76
D A Prince *This house*	77
William Letford *Marriage*	79

Illustrations

Michelle Templeton *Tea Kettle*	Front endpaper
Howard Phipps *Sunlit Doorway*	11
Anne Hayward *As the Light Changes*	15
John O'Connor *Teacup*	17
Clifford Harper *Kneading Dough*	19
Mary Azarian *Summer Kitchen*	21
Jonathan Mercer *Prix Fixe*	23
Rebecca Gryspeerdt *Boy under Piano*	25
Howard Phipps *Cottage Interior*	27
Michelle Templeton *Tea Kettle*	29
John O'Connor *Canals, Barges and People*	33
Yvonne Skargon *Cat on Sofa*	35
Elspeth Robertson *Attic Studio*	37
Anita Klein *Girl with Candle*	40
Violet Moore Higgins *Girl in Bed*	43
Rosalind Atkins *Pantry*	45
Howard Phipps *Sunlit Interior*	48
Mary Azarian *Domestic Angel*	50
Four Girls in the Kitchen having a Tea Party	52
Howard Phipps *Interior Manor Farm*	56
Howard Phipps *The Workroom Window*	61
John O'Connor *Chair*	65
Jonathan Mercer *When the Day*	69
Howard Phipps *Kitchen Garden Doorway*	73
Miriam Macgregor *Barnsley House*	77
Bob Guy *Back Door*	Back endpaper

Scaffolding

Seamus Heaney (1939-1913)

Masons, when they start upon a building,
Are careful to test out the scaffolding;

Make sure that planks won't slip at busy points,
Secure all ladders, tighten bolted joints.

And yet all this comes down when the job's done
Showing off walls of sure and solid stone.

So if, my dear, there sometimes seem to be
Old bridges breaking between you and me

Never fear. We may let the scaffolds fall
Confident that we have built our wall.

A Ballad of Home

Eavan Boland

How we kissed
in our half built-house!
It was slightly timbered,
a bit bricked, on stilts

and we were newly married.
We drove out at dusk
and picked our way to safety
through flint and grit and brick.

Like water through a porthole,
the sky poured in.
We sat on one step
making estimations

and hugged until the watchman
called and cursed and swung
his waterproof torch
into our calculations.

Ten years on:
you wouldn't find now
an inch of spare ground.
Children in their cots,

books, a cat, plants
strain the walls' patience
and the last ounce of space.
And still every night

it all seems so sound.
But love why wouldn't it?
This house was built on our embrace
and there are worse foundations.

The Door

Charles Tomlinson (1927-2015)

Too little
has been said
of the door, its one
face turned to the night's
downpour and its other
to the shift and glisten of firelight.

Air, clasped
by this cover
into the room's book,
is filled by the turning
pages of dark and fire
as the wind shoulders the panels, or unsteadies that burning.

Not only
the storm's
breakwater, but the sudden
frontier to our concurrences, appearances
and as full of the offer of space
as the view through a cromlech is.

For doors
are both frame and monument
to our spent time,
and too little
has been said
of our coming through and leaving by them.

The cromlech in this poem is a prehistoric structure, stone uprights and a block of stone on top, looking rather like a doorway in, say, the open landscape of Wales – the author.

The first warm morning
Esther Morgan

I move through the house
opening windows stiff as joints
after months of rain.

Curtains lacy with sunlight
gesture into an empty room.
Sounds enter on the air:

an occasional car passing,
the clink of tools renovating,
a playground's archive of laughter.

This Room

Imtiaz Dharker

This room is breaking out
of itself, cracking through
its own walls in search of space, light,
empty air.

The bed is lifting out of
its nightmares.
From dark corners, chairs
are rising up to crash through clouds.

This is the time and place
to be alive:
when the daily furniture of our lives
stirs, when the improbable arrives.
Pots and pans bang together
in celebration, clang
past the crowd of garlic, onions, spices,
fly by the ceiling fan.
No one is looking for the door.

In all this excitement
I'm wondering where
I've left my feet, and why

my hands are outside, clapping.

Home
Esme

After all the harsh and slow weariness.
After all the unbearable battle. The trudge and the grudge and the awful tread.
I burst open a door and burst into a hot, salty fountain. The change of clothes.
The twirl around the warm bright room. The smiles. The relief. The freedom.
The smell of the familiar.
The sight of the bright.
The taste of something good.
The feel of a hug.
And the warmth, the glorious warmth.
The twinkle.
The generosity.
The glorious, glorious, freedom
Of never watching my back.
And, of course,
The joy.

Table
Robert Hull

We were going to sell the table.
It's big where it is,
with those elbowing edges
coming after us
and corners
that force us into corners.

But we decided not to. Instead,
we said,
we'd rub down the surface,
get rid of each burn and dent
and moon of stain
and the stuck inch of newsprint.

But we've not even been able
to start cleaning our old table.

It had too many babies
changed on it,
too many trumpets
and spoons whanged on it,
too many whales and witches
drawn on it
to do anything with it;

there's been too much homework and grief
dumped on it, too much laughter
heard round it, too many candles
burned down over it,
to do anything else but leave it there,
in the awkward place it's in,

elbowing us with its edges,
reminding us.

Camomile Tea

Katherine Mansfield (1888-1923)

Outside the sky is light with stars;
There's a hollow roaring from the sea.
And, alas! for the little almond flowers,
The wind is shaking the almond tree.

How little I thought, a year ago,
In the horrible cottage upon the Lee
That he and I should be sitting so
And sipping a cup of camomile tea.

Light as feathers the witches fly,
The horn of the moon is plain to see;
By a firefly under a jonquil flower
A goblin toasts a bumble-bee.

We might be fifty, we might be five,
So snug, so compact, so wise are we!
Under the kitchen-table leg
My knee is pressing against his knee.

Our shutters are shut, the fire is low,
The tap is dripping peacefully;
The saucepan shadows on the wall
Are black and round and plain to see.

Cups

Gwen Harwood (1920-1995)

They know us by our lips. They know the proverb
about the space between us. Many slip.
They are older than their flashy friends, the glasses.
They held water first, are named in scripture.

Most are gregarious. You'll often see them
nestled in snowy flocks on trestle tables
or perched on trolleys. Quite a few stay married
for life in their own home to the same saucer,

and some are virgin brides of quietness
in a parlour cupboard, wearing gold and roses.
Handless, chipped, some live on in the flour bin,
some with the poisons in the potting shed.

Shattered, they lie in flowerpot, flowerbed, fowlyard.
Fine earth in earth, they wait for resurrection.
Restored, unbreakable, they'll meet our lips
on some bright morning filled with lovingkindness.

When I Am in the Kitchen

Jeanne Marie Beaumont

I think about the past. I empty the ice-cube trays
crack crack cracking like bones, and I think
of decades of ice cubes and of John Cheever,
of Anne Sexton making cocktails, of decades
of cocktail parties, and it feels suddenly far
too lonely at my counter. Although I have on hooks
nearby the embroidered apron of my friend's
grandmother and one my mother made for me
for Christmas 30 years ago with gingham I had
coveted through my childhood. In my kitchen
I wield my great aunt's sturdy black-handled
soup ladle and spatula, and when I pull out
the drawer, like one in a morgue, I visit
the silverware of my husband's grandparents.
We never met, but I place this in my mouth
every day and keep it polished out of duty.
In the cabinets I find my godmother's
teapot, my mother's Cambridge glass goblets,
my mother-in-law's Franciscan plates, and here
is the cutting board my first husband parqueted
and two potholders I wove in grade school.
Oh the past is too much with me in the kitchen,
where I open the vintage metal recipe box,
robin's egg blue in its interior, to uncover
the card for Waffles, writ in my father's hand
reaching out from the grave to guide me
from the beginning, "sift and mix dry ingredients"
with his note that this makes "3 waffles in our
large pan" and around that *our* an unbearable
round stain—of egg yolk or melted butter?—
that once defined a world.

Daily Bread

Jane Clarke

A white mist rises as she sifts a pound of flour
into the worn, tin basin, wide as Lough Corrib.

Blue veins lie like rivers on the map of her hands.
She measures one teaspoon of bread soda,

two teaspoons of salt. The plait at the nape
of her neck: a fisherman's rope coiled at the quay.

She scoops a hollow, pours a pint of buttermilk,
splashing and spluttering into the well.

With the rhythm of a rower she kneads rough dough
on the flour-dusted table, pushing it away,

pulling it back, pushing it away again.
With her wrist she flicks a lock, silver-grey frost

in December, from her high cheek bones. Readying
the bread for its hot harbour, she cuts a deep cross.

Wooden Spoons
Nina Bogin

If spoons have souls it's because
our hands have burnished them
with the warmth of our grip

mingling with the seasons
embedded in their grain.
Upright in a pitcher

like a stand of trees in winter,
they still weather the passage of time.
Take this spoon, its handle warped,

the chipped edge of its scoop
in a lopsided smile – it's the one
I reach for when I stir the soup,

curved to my palm, my gestures.
Does the spoon know me as I know it?
Sometimes it knows me too well.

I see you in the kitchen
peeling apples and quinces,
cooking compote in a saucepan –

as if tasks outlived us.
As if I took the stirring spoon
from your hand.

Home
Dennis O'Driscoll (1954-2012)

when all is said and done
what counts is having someone
you can phone at five to ask

for the immersion heater
to be switched to 'bath'
and the pizza taken from the deepfreeze

Dinner with my Mother

Hugo Williams

My mother is saying 'Now'.
'Now,' she says, taking down a saucepan,
putting it on the stove.
She doesn't say anything else for a while,

so that time passes slowly, on the simmer,
until it is 'Now' again
as she hammers out our steaks
for Steak Diane.

I have to be on hand at times like this
for table-laying,
drink replenishment
and general conversational encouragement,

but I am getting hungry
and there is nowhere to sit down.
'Now,' I say, making a point
of opening a bottle of wine.

My mother isn't listening.
She's miles away,
testing the sauce with a spoon,
narrowing her eyes through the steam.

'Now', she says very slowly, meaning
which is it to be,
the rosemary or the tarragon vinegar
for the salad dressing?

I hold my breath, lest anything
should go wrong at the last minute.
But now it is really 'Now',
our time to sit and eat.

Zenith

Ted Kooser

It was part of her parlor's darkness
during the war years – its Gothic cabinet,
its shadowy speaker behind a thin lattice
like the face of a priest – but when
my grandmother snapped its switch
each evening to tune in the news,
it opened the tiny Japanese fan
of its dial and light spilled over her fingers,
swollen and stiff. And in the near darkness
my sister and I, shushed into silence,
and Grandmother, rubbing and kneading
the pain from her hands, sat there
at the rear of the action, a patrol
in the weak yellow glow from the war.

Piano

D H Lawrence (1885-1930)

Softly, in the dusk, a woman is singing to me;
Taking me back down the vista of years, till I see
A child sitting under the piano, in the boom of the tingling strings
And pressing the small, poised feet of a mother who smiles as she sings.

In spite of myself, the insidious mastery of song
Betrays me back, till the heart of me weeps to belong
To the old Sunday evenings at home, with winter outside
And hymns in the cosy parlour, the tinkling piano our guide.

So now it is vain for the singer to burst into clamour
With the great black piano appassionato. The glamour
Of childish days is upon me, my manhood is cast
Down in the flood of remembrance, I weep like a child for the past.

The Kitchen Table

In memory of my Mother
Clive Wilmer

Making a home was
what you could do
best, and cookery

(the ritual at
the heart of it) you had
a kind of genius for.

So what I first
recall, thinking of you,
is a creamy table-top,

the grain etched
crude and deep, the legs
stained black, and you

at work, with rolling-pin
or chopping-board or
bowl; then later

presiding over
guests or children at each
day's informal feast.

Your homeliness
displaced now, what survives
for me of it

is this: which
now becomes a model
of true art:

bare boards scrubbed clean,
black, white,
good work as grace, such

purity of heart.

In the Kitchen
Penelope Shuttle

A jug of water
has its own lustrous turmoil

The ironing board thanks god
for its two good strong legs and sturdy back

The new fridge hums like a maniac
with helpfulness

I am trying to love the world
back to normal

The chair recites its stand-alone prayer
again and again

The table leaves no stone unturned
The clock votes for the separate burial of hearts

I am trying to love the world
and all its 8,000 identifiable languages

With the forgetfulness of a potter
I'm trying to get the seas back on the maps
where they belong

secured to their rivers

The kettle alone knows the good he does,
Here in the kitchen, loving the world,
Steadfastly loving

See how easy it is, he whistles

A Winter Morning

Ted Kooser

A farmhouse window far back from the highway
speaks to the darkness in a small, sure voice.
Against this stillness, only a kettle's whisper,
And against the starry cold, one small blue ring of flame.

Guests
Cynthia Fuller

Awe at the first arrival,
they turned up with wet plastered hair
faces flattened by travel,

journey's end the heart centre.
They stayed, settled in
grew familiar, departed.

Years of living together
concentrate down to a weekend visit
lit by anticipation,

the most honoured guests
for whom dishes, towels, sheets
are embellished with love.

Visit over
a phone call sets them
safe in their grown up lives.

Silence has changed into
absence of voice,
the small house too spacious,

washing and folding
to pack love away again
hard to find room on the shelf.

Let a Place be Made

Yves Bonnefoy (1923-2016)
Translated by Anthony Rudolf

Let a place be made for the one who draws near,
The one who is cold, deprived of any home,

Tempted by the sound of a lamp, by the lit
Threshold of a solitary house.

And if he is still exhausted, full of anguish,
Say again for him the words that heal.

What does this heart which once was silence need
If not those words which are both sign and prayer,

Like a fire caught sight of in the sudden night,
Like the table glimpsed in a poor house?

Teapot

Beverley Bie Brahic

Daughters are the guardians of memory,
said *Belle-maman*, spooning bread with honey.

– And why not sons? But to her daughters
she left the linens, darned with memories.

I've flown home from the other country, over
my native provinces the colour of honey.

Farewell for a while to the rented condo,
kitchen cupboards unfurnished with memories.

I lift the teapot – the Aladdin-shaped one –
down from the shelf, and the jar of honey.

A wedding gift. Often dropped. Lid askew,
pewter blotched. The soft cloth of memory

makes it a lamp on the dullest day, as mirror
with tarnished silvering. I drizzle honey

over my bread. Kettle chirps. I warm the pot.
I steep verbena in the teapot of memory.

What if I swaddle it like a hot water bottle,
pack it up with a jar of the lavender honey,

fly it some Great Circle Route back to Silicon Valley,
my kitchen cupboards, bare of memories.

Then, if I fly northeast again, over
my native forests, prairies and honey,

I'll leave it with my son – no – my daughter:
daughters are the guardians of memory,

and my son will fall in love with another woman
(I see her already; she's a honey)

and will she, won't she
care for my memories?

The Sofa

Jehane Markham

A woman full of hope comes home
She puts her bag on the sofa
Her bag spills open and out tumbles her phone.
She puts down the shape of her step-daughter asleep on the sofa
The night her daddy died.
Then she lays down the feeling of arms around her
While Liane Carrol sings the blues.
She smells aftershave on the cushions.
She puts down the anguish of loss and the enclosure of family.
Her book falls open on the sofa.
She puts down forgetfulness and erasure.
She wishes she could dance all night
And sleep like a baby in a goose feather bed.
She adds up 30 plus 9 and puts 39 on the sofa.
She puts down all her favourite songs
And hears them singing in her head.
She crumples a photo of herself looking at him
While he holds the baby.
She lays down the ghost of a man
Who said he never stopped loving her
Though sometimes it felt like he did.
The sofa is feeling the weight
Of all this emotion
It sinks a bit but it doesn't give way.

A Sofa in the Forties

(first verse)
Seamus Heaney (1939-2013)

All of us on the sofa in a line, kneeling
Behind each other, eldest down to youngest.
Elbows going like pistons, for this was a train

And between the jamb-wall and the bedroom door
Our speed and distance were inestimable.
First we shunted, then we whistled, then

Somebody collected the invisible
For tickets and very gravely punched it
As carriage after carriage under us

Moved faster, *chooka-chook*, the sofa legs
Went giddy and the unreachable ones
Far out on the kitchen floor began to wave.

Hearth

D A Prince

My mother had the trick of it
holding a broadsheet page (*The Cambrian News*)
against the leaded grate. She made it fit
tight on the hood, stretched above sullen coals,
kneeling, her fingers fanned out, pulling taut
the papers risk. Behind the melting print
we'd hear that first shy crack as kindling caught,
then flickered louder. Still she knelt
holding the glow, hiding the heat until
just as the newsprint scorched, she pulled it back.

A solid flame roared up. The chimney gulped.
The coals sang in their scarlet surplices.
A stubby poker gleamed.

                        Then the browned page
biscuit-crisp and folded, tucked by the fender
for tomorrow's turn. *Don't touch*, she warned,
growing the fire to draw us closer in.

Winter Heart

Jackie Kay

My love, the nights are coming now in the afternoons,
and it is nearly the time of year when everyone wonders
where they should be and with whom;
and you are in the room –

all full of heart on your face and your sleeve –
your lovely face open as the spring, in the winter
evening with the dark coming down like a good soul song –
'Darling, you send me, honest you do.'

So, maybe, stoke up the fire in the living room,
and light the long candles. Hold me close
while the stars outside shiver and spell out their names –
bright as any love, anywhere, any time.

An Amish Rug
Michael Longley

As if a one-room schoolhouse were all we knew
And our clothes were black, our underclothes black,
Marriage a horse and buggy going to church
And the children silhouettes in a snowy field,

I bring you this patchwork like a smallholding
Where I served as the hired boy behind the harrow,
Its threads the colour of cantaloupe and cherry
Securing hay bales, corn cobs, tobacco leaves.

You may hang it on the wall, a cathedral window,
Or lay it out on the floor beside our bed
So that whenever we undress for sleep or love
We shall step over it as over a flowerbed.

Anne Hathaway
Carol Ann Duffy

Item I gyve unto my wief my second best bed...'
(from Shakespeare's will)

The bed we loved in was a spinning world
of forests, castles, torchlight, cliff-tops, seas
where he would dive for pearls. My lover's words
were shooting stars which fell to earth as kisses
on these lips; my body now a softer rhyme
to his, now echo, assonance; his touch
a verb dancing in the centre of a noun.
Some nights I dreamed he'd written me, the bed
a page beneath his writer's hands. Romance
and drama played by touch, by scent, by taste.
In the other bed, the best, our guests dozed on,
dribbling their prose. My living laughing love –
I hold him in the casket of my widow's head
as he held me upon that next best bed.

from **Figs and Thistles: First Fig**
by Edna St Vincent Millay (1892-1950)

My candle burns at both ends;
It will not last the night;
But ah, my foes, and oh, my friends –
It gives a lovely light!

The Candle

Katherine Mansfield (1888-1923)

By my bed, on a little round table,
The Grandmother placed a candle.
She gave me three kisses telling me they were three dreams
And tucked me in just where I loved being tucked.
Then she went out of the room and the door was shut.
I lay still, waiting for my three dreams to talk;
But they were silent.
Suddenly I remembered giving her three kisses back.
Perhaps, by mistake, I had given my three little dreams.
I sat up in bed.
The room grew big, oh, bigger far than a church.
The wardrobe, quite by itself, as big as a house.
And the jug on the washstand smiled at me:
It was not a friendly smile.
I looked at the basket-chair where my clothes lay folded:
The chair gave a creak as though it were listening for something.
Perhaps it was coming alive and going to dress in my clothes.
But the awful thing was the window:
I could not think what was outside.
No tree to be seen, I was sure,
No nice little plant or friendly pebbly path.
Why did she pull the blind down every night?
It was better to know.
I crunched my teeth and crept out of bed.
I peeped through a slit of blind.
There was nothing at all to be seen
But hundreds of friendly candles all over the sky
In remembrance of frightened children.
I went back to bed…
The three dreams started singing a little song.

Sky Canoe

Deryn Rees-Jones

"I see, not feel, how beautiful they are."
Samuel Taylor Coleridge

Sometimes this bed without love, this
settling to sleep like children,
hand-in-hand, knees fitted into knees,
the radio on low, our books, clothes,
daily lives strewn carelessly about the floor

is both more and less than I can bear.
Take this sky the night has given us —
not the Pleiades or the Seven Sisters,
Cassiopeia with her train of hair —
but a heaven we have made ourselves,
the bright planets of our bedroom firmament

glow-in-the-dark plastic stars
fixed to a painted square.

Bed

Anon

Covers pulled up
Love-worn rabbit in my arms
My bed paradise.

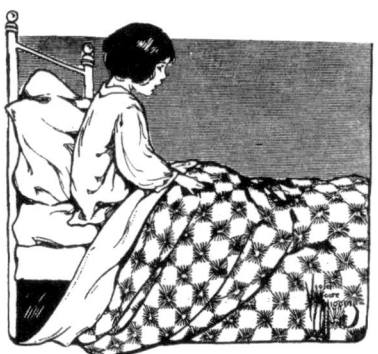

Midnight in the Pantry

Edgar Guest (1881-1959)

You can boast your round of pleasures, praise the sound of popping corks,
Where the orchestra is playing to the rattle of the forks,
And your after-opera dinner you may think superbly fine,
But that can't compare, I'm certain, to the joy that's always mine
When I reach my little dwelling—source, of all sincere delight—
And I prowl around the pantry in the waning hours of night.
When my business, or my pleasure, has detained me until late,
And it's midnight, say, or after, when I reach my own estate,
Though I'm weary with my toiling I don't hustle up to bed,
For the inner man is hungry and he's anxious to be fed,
Then I feel a thrill of glory from my head down to my feet
As I prowl around the pantry after something good to eat.
Oft I hear a call above me: 'Goodness gracious, come to bed!'
And I know that I've disturbed her by my overeager tread,
But I've found a glass of jelly and some bread and butter, too,
And a bit of cold fried chicken and I answer: 'When I'm through!'
Oh, there's no café that better serves my precious appetite
Than the pantry in our kitchen when I get home late at night.
You may boast your shining silver, and the linen and the flowers,
And the music and the laughter and the lights that hang in showers,
You may have your café table with its brilliant array,
But it doesn't charm yours truly when I'm on my homeward way,
For a greater joy awaits me, as I hunger for a bite—
Just the joy of pantry-prowling in the middle of the night.

Spice Jars

D A Prince

They stood for years, high on the pantry shelf.
Then dust to dust: loose stoppers, grey and furred,
greasy with age, neglect, the labels blurred,
each spice surrendering its ancient self
turned pensioner-apologetic, yet
leaving a perfect circle clean when lifted
like some domestic chess piece shifted
in one last game, or stately minuet.

I opened one: faint kitchen scents (a trace
of fruit breads, Welsh cakes, and the kitchen warm
and welcoming from school) took shadow form:
allspice and nutmeg, cinnamon and mace,
caraway for seed cakes or for loaves,
and dry, black-budded rattlings of cloves.

This Is Just to Say
William Carlos Williams

I have eaten
the plums
that were in
the icebox

and which
you were probably
saving
for breakfast

Forgive me
they were delicious
so sweet
and so cold

Tango
Beverley Bie Brahic

Waiting for the porridge pot to boil
I practice Argentine tango
Extending first one leg, then the second;
And the silver kettle's gravid belly
Mirrors me in my blue nightgown:
My spine is straight, my arms curve round
As if to hold a beach ball
Or that red balloon the sun
Just rising from the puzzled rooftops.
One street over I see a girl
Jump to catch a string she never
Thought could slip away so fast...

> *Mind what you're doing, or you'll fall!*
> *Move your right foot forward,*
> *Brush your left instep; flex*
> *Your knees the way Natasha said...*

Natasha Ng from Buenos Aires,
Who won't allow us to *Embrace*
Or dance *Cruzada* and *Boleo*
Until we learn to walk. *Caminar.*
Sun floods the room in the kettle:
Slotted spoon, plate of fruit, the copper scales
To weigh and measure
From my husband's mother's Marseille pharmacy;
We could be a portrait, I think,
A Picture of a Woman in a Kettle.

The Slicing of Carrots
David Scott (1947-2022)

Legs tucked satisfactorily under her
she was at ease with the stone floor.
For most of it was the time of resting.
The still kitchen hung in the balance
of the day. The light was pressed
through only one of the doors,
the other being shut. I could see
the slicing of carrots produced a pile
of saffron-coloured shards. Light
and dark seemed more so and tighter
for being opposites. The shot-through silk
of her sari, and the shape and rhyme of the duty,
seemed right for one content to work.
The peace that came with the soul of the place
in which it was done, shared her beauty.
Beauty and light seemed something
she both wore, and won.

This Morning
Esther Morgan

I watched the sun moving round the kitchen,
an early spring sun that strengthened and weakened,
coming and going like an old mind.

I watched like one bedridden for a long time
on their first journey back into the world
who finds it enough to be going on with:

the way the sunlight brought each possession in turn
to its attention and made of it a small still life:

the iron frying pan gleaming on its hook like an ancient find,
the powdery green cheek of a bruised clementine.

Though more beautiful still was how the light moved on,
letting go each chair and coffee cup without regret

the way my grandmother, in her final year, received me:
neither surprised by my presence, nor distressed by my leaving,
content, though, while I was there.

Woman Work

(first verse)
Maya Angelou (1928-2014)

I've got the children to tend
The clothes to mend
The floor to mop
The food to shop
Then the chicken to fry
The baby to dry
I got company to feed
The garden to weed
I've got shirts to press
The tots to dress
The cane to be cut
I gotta clean up this hut
Then see about the sick
And the cotton to pick.

Canning
Joyce Sutphen

It's what she does and what her mother did.
It's what I'd do if I were anything
like her mother's mother—or if the times
demanded that I work in my garden,
planting rows of beans and carrots, weeding
the pickles and potatoes, picking worms
off the cabbages.   Today she's canning
tomatoes, which means there are baskets
of red Jubilees waiting on the porch
and she's been in the cellar looking for jars.
There's a box of lids and a heap of gold
rings on the counter. She gets the spices
out; she revs the engine of the old stove.

Now I declare her Master of Preserves!
I say that if there were degrees in canning
she would be *summa cum laude*—God knows
she's spent as many hours at the sink peeling
the skins off hot tomatoes as I have
bent over a difficult text. I see
her at the window, filling up the jar,
packing a glass suitcase for the winter.

Polly put the kettle on
Anon

Polly put the kettle on,
Polly put the kettle on,
Polly put the kettle on,
We'll all have tea.

Sukey take it off again,
Sukey take it off again,
Sukey take it off again,
They've all gone away.

Setting the Table

Dorothy Aldis (1896-1966)

Evenings
When the house is quiet
I delight
To spread the white
Smooth cloth and put the flowers on the table.

I place the knives and forks around
Without a sound.
I light the candles.

I love to see
Their small reflected torches shine
Against the greenness of the vine
And garden.

Is that the mignonette, I wonder,
Smells so sweet?

And then I call them in to eat.

Table

Edip Cansever (1928-1986)
Translated from the Turkish by Julia Clare Tillinghast and Richard Tillinghast

A man filled with the gladness of living
Put his keys on the table,
Put flowers in a copper bowl there.
He put his eggs and milk on the table.
He put there the light that came in through the window,
Sound of a bicycle, sound of a spinning wheel.
The softness of bread and weather he put there.
On the table the man put
Things that happened in his mind.
What he wanted to do in life,
He put that there.
Those he loved, those he didn't love,
The man put them on the table too.
Three times three make nine:
The man put nine on the table.
He was next to the window next to the sky;
He reached out and placed on the table endlessness.
So many days he had wanted to drink a beer!
He put on the table the pouring of that beer.
He placed there his sleep and his wakefulness;
His hunger and his fullness he put there.
Now that's what I call a table!
It didn't complain at all about the load.
It wobbled once or twice, then stood firm.
The man kept piling things on.

Setting

Rosemerry Wahtola Trommer

In every conversation
there is a table made of listening.
Sometimes the tables are beautiful,
solid, clean—the kind
that can support anything
you put on them.
Sometimes, they're like
the tv dinner trays
of my childhood—
a little rickety, but they'll do
if what's put on them is light.
Sometimes they're so cluttered
that whatever's placed on their surface
is almost immediately lost.
Let tonight's table have a small vase of flowers
and a candle perhaps, nothing else.
May it be small enough we might
see each other's eyes, might notice
every nuance of breath. Whomever
I am most nervous to invite,
may I invite them. And though
the tea is just a metaphor,
may I offer. May they accept.

Night Piece

Osip Mandelstam (1891-1938)
Translated by Christian Wiman

Come love let us sit together
In the cramped kitchen breathing kerosene.
There's fuel enough to forget the weather,
The knife is ours and the bread is clean.

Come love let us play the game
Of what to take and when to run,
Of come with me and come what may
And holding hands to hold off the sun.

Wind

Ted Hughes (1930-1998)

This house has been far out at sea all night,
The woods crashing through darkness, the booming hills,
Winds stampeding the fields under the window
Floundering black astride and blinding wet

Till day rose; then under an orange sky
The hills had new places, and wind wielded
Blade-light, luminous black and emerald,
Flexing like the lens of a mad eye.

At noon I scaled along the house-side as far as
The coal-house door. Once I looked up –
Through the brunt wind that dented the balls of my eyes
The tent of the hills drummed and strained its guyrope,

The fields quivering, the skyline a grimace,
At any second to bang and vanish with a flap;
The wind flung a magpie away and a black-
Back gull bent like an iron bar slowly. The house

Rang like some fine green goblet in the note
That any second would shatter it. Now deep
In chairs, in front of the great fire, we grip
Our hearts and cannot entertain book, thought,

Or each other. We watch the fire blazing,
And feel the roots of the house move, but sit on,
Seeing the window tremble to come in,
Hearing the stones cry out under the horizons.

Being Boring

Wendy Cope

'May you live in interesting times.' Chinese curse

If you ask me 'What's new?', I have nothing to say
Except that the garden is growing.
I had a slight cold but it's better today.
I'm content with the way things are going.
Yes, he is the same as he usually is,
Still eating and sleeping and snoring.
I get on with my work. He gets on with his.
I know this is all very boring.

There was drama enough in my turbulent past:
Tears and passion – I've used up a tankful.
No news is good news, and long may it last.
If nothing much happens, I'm thankful.
A happier cabbage you never did see,
My vegetable spirits are soaring.
If you're after excitement, steer well clear of me.
I want to go on being boring.

I don't go to parties. Well, what are they for,
If you don't need to find a new lover?
You drink and you listen and drink a bit more
And you take the next day to recover.
Someone to stay home with was all my desire
And, now that I've found a safe mooring,
I've just one ambition in life: I aspire
To go on and on being boring.

A Rainy Sunday

Ruby Archer (1873-1961)

I love a rainy Sunday,
With all the world away;
The cozy hearth intensified
By gloom of outer day.

In silken gown fantastic,
I let my hair go free,
And idle in and out of books,
Or weave a melody.

The rain beyond the window
Chants on in monotone;
I muse among my household gods,
And laugh—to be alone.

The family is drowsy,
The very cat asleep;
And naught comes nigh my revery,
Growing in silence deep.

My books are dear companions,
My pictures well-loved friends,
My brown divan with Orient grace
A dreamy languor lends.

Come often, rainy Sundays,
Forbidding me to roam—
Come often, shut the world without,
And me within my home.

Desk Duty

Hugo Williams

My desk has brought me
all my worst fears on a big tray
and left it across my lap.
I'm not allowed to move until I have
eaten everything up.
I push things around on my plate.
I kick the heating pipes.

A piece of worn carpet on the floor
proves how long I've been sitting here
shuffling my feet,
opening and closing drawers,
looking for something I've lost
under piles of official papers and threats,
roofing grants and housing benefits.

Am I married or single?
Employed or self-employed?
What sort of work do I do?
Is my house being used for business
or entertainment purposes? (See Note 3)
If I am resident at my place of work,
who supplies the furniture?

I have cause to suspect myself
of deliberately wasting time
writing my name and place of birth
under 'Who else lives with you?'
It has taken me all day
to find something true to write
under 'Personal Allowances' – or not untrue.

I know all about my little game
of declaring more than I earn
to the Inland Revenue – or was it less?
I'm guilty as hell,
or I wouldn't be sitting here like this
playing footy-footy with my desk.
I'd be upstairs in bed with my bed.

Instructions for a Bookcase

Catherine Flynn

Stand up straight.
Keep your shelves long and strong;
Don't let them sag!
Hold each book in a gentle hug,
Protect covers from fading,
Prevent dust from settling on pages,
Preserve words, ideas, stories.
Welcome every reader;
Generously share your treasures.

The Chair

John Fuller

This is my chair. From which I reach
To feed the logs with the pale blue aura
Of some biscuit foil,
Elusive afterthought,
Flower of a fiery soil.

It is a cradle of supposition,
Receiving me as the stove receives
Its butchered kin,
A fierce intensity
To be consumed within.

And if thought possess its hour of blooming
Between the cooling teapot, say,
Glazed on its rivet
And the golden promise of
A finger of Glenlivet

It is by permission of such treats
That I can blaze with the simple idea
Of a locus where
There is very little to think
But this: this is my chair.

Year of the Hen

Margaret Atwood

This is the year of sorting,
of throwing out, of giving back,
of sifting through the heaps, the piles,
the drifts, the dunes, the sediments,

or less poetically, the shelves, the trunks,
the closets, boxes, corners
in the cellar, nooks and cupboards –

the junk, in other words,
that's blown in here, or else been saved,
or else has eddied, or been thrown
my way by unseen waves.

For instance: two thick layers
of blank glass jars that once held jam
we made in those evaporated
summers; a frugal slew
of plastic bags; a cracked maroon umbrella
so prized when new;

a chocolate box with crayon ends
stored up for phantom children;
shoes with the grimy marks
of toes that once were mine.
Photos of boys whose names are lost
(posing so jauntily in front of chrome-
trimmed cars), many of them
dead now, the others old –

everything speckled and faded, jumbled
together like – let's say – this bowl
of miscellaneous pebbles gathered
time after time on beaches now
eroded or misplaced, but scooped up then
and fingered for their beauty,
and pocketed as pure mementoes
of some once indelible day.

Home
Mahendra Solanki

I am at home here, among
the priest's paraphernalia:
the incense, the tulsi leaves,
carefully measured amounts
of rice, flour, cotton, saffron
threads; items from a prescribed
list, long rehearsed with newly-
found aunts and long-lost uncles.

It's what brings us back to earth,
another ritual, at home.

tulsi – holy basil

Inside My Zulu Hut

Oswald Mbuyiseni Mtshali

It is a hive
without any bees
to build the walls
with golden bricks of honey.
A cave cluttered
with a millstone,
calabashes of sour milk
claypots of foaming beer
sleeping grass mats

wooden head rests
tanned goat skins
tied with riempies
to wattle rafters
blackened by the smoke
of kneaded cow dung
burning under
the three-legged pot
on the earthen floor
to cook my porridge.

calabashes – gourds
riempies – strips of rawhide or leather, used as a rope or in making chairs and other furniture

Home
Edward Thomas (1878-1917)

Often I had gone this way before:
But now it seemed I never could be
And never had been anywhere else;
'Twas home; one nationality
We had, I and the birds that sang,
One memory.

They welcomed me. I had come back
That eve somehow from somewhere far:
The April mist, the chill, the calm,
Meant the same thing familiar
And pleasant to us, and strange too,
Yet with no bar.

The thrush on the oaktop in the lane
Sang his last song, or last but one;
And as he ended, on the elm
Another had but just begun
His last; they knew no more than I
The day was done.

Then past his dark white cottage front
A labourer went along, his tread
Slow, half with weariness, half with ease;
And, through the silence, from his shed
The sound of sawing rounded all
That silence said.

Home
xx. Homecoming

Jim Carruth

Never lose this hunger for home.
At the end of the day
after long labour in the fields,
backache and setting sun,
you descend the hill again,
soul-tired with heavy steps,
a weariness that buckles legs
from honest hours. Knowing
you could have done no more
you watch for a kindling of lights,
for smoke rising from the first fires;
at our feet, collies swim the dusk.
After all this time you could find
your way back blind.

Autumn River Song

Li T'ai-po (701-762)
Translated by Hami

The moon shimmers in green water.
White herons fly through the moonlight.

The young man hears a girl gathering water-chestnuts:
into the night, singing, they paddle home together.

The Fruit Garden Path

Amy Lowell (1874-1925)

The path runs straight between the flowering rows,
A moonlit path, hemmed in by beds of bloom,
Where phlox and marigolds dispute for room
With tall, red dahlias and the briar rose.
'T is reckless prodigality which throws
Into the night these wafts of rich perfume
Which sweep across the garden like a plume.
Over the trees a single bright star glows.
Dear garden of my childhood, here my years
Have run away like little grains of sand;
The moments of my life, its hopes and fears
Have all found utterance here, where now I stand;
My eyes ache with the weight of unshed tears,
You are my home, do you not understand?

Prayer
Carol Ann Duffy

Some days, although we cannot pray, a prayer
utters itself. So, a woman will lift
her head from the sieve of her hands and stare
at the minims sung by a tree, a sudden gift.

Some nights, although we are faithless, the truth
enters our hearts, that small familiar pain;
then a man will stand stock-still, hearing his youth
in the distant Latin chanting of a train.

Pray for us now. Grade 1 piano scales
console the lodger looking out across
a Midlands town. Then dusk, and someone calls
a child's name as though they named their loss.

Darkness outside. Inside, the radio's prayer -
Rockall. Malin. Dogger. Finisterre.

An Expedition
Peter Didsbury

Down to the end of the garden in the night.
With cigarette and glass of ice-cold milk.
I pick my way over heaps of builders' rubble.
Light from the new kitchen window comes along too.

Leaf-huts and Snow-houses

Olav H Hauge
Translated from the Norwegian by Robin Fulton

There's not much to
these verses, only
a few words piled up
at random.
I think
nonetheless
it's fine
to make them, then
for a little while
I have something like a house.
I remember leaf-huts
we built
when we were small:
to creep in and sit
listening to the rain,
feel alone in the wilderness,
drops on your nose
and your hair –
Or snow-houses at Christmas,
to creep in and
close the hole with a sack,
light a candle and stay there
on cold evenings.

Lattice
Grace Wells

Come, I said to the creatures, nest,
drey, burrow, warren, set.

Come briar, weave a covert for fox.
Come willow knit an earth for badger.

Grass, grow tall enough for hare's form,
safe enough for the leverets in spring.

Come, I said to the creatures, return,
while I live, you will be safe on this half-acre.

Who have we been with our evictions?
Poor landlords. Drunk squanderers.
We have gambled our fortune.

Burrow neighbouring bolt-hole,
beside rhizome, beneath lair.

Frogspawn to pool. Salmon gilt to the stream.
Eel to the river. Hawk to the hill.

Come home, I called to the species.
Let us build a lattice of shelters close on one another.
Let us restore the matrix of home.

Sonnet XXXIII

Pablo Neruda (1904-1973)
Translated by Stephen Tapscott

Love, we're going home now,
where the vines clamber over the trellis:
even before you, the summer will arrive,
on its honeysuckle feet, in your bedroom.

Our nomadic kisses wandered over all the world:
Armenia, dollop of disinterred honey–:
Ceylon, green dove–: and the Yang-Tse with its old
old patience, dividing the day from the night.

And now, dearest, we return, across the crackling sea
like two blind birds to their wall,
To their nest in a distant spring:

because love cannot always fly without resting,
our lives return to the wall, to the rocks of the sea:
our kisses head back home where they belong.

This house
D A Prince

loves summer, loves
doors all-day stretching to hot lawns, loves
yawning windows, loves
slow hammock-swing of curtains, loves
spiralling child-pitch of voices, loves
hay-smells and pollen, loves
its cool and shadowed kitchen, loves
lemons and cucumbers, garden berries, loves
crack of heat in its joists, loves
arthritic easings, creak of wooden weight, loves
shuttered corners with the lazy buzz of bees, loves
the calendar of visits, loves
lavender and butterflies, loves
itself.

Acknowledgements

We would like to thank Neil Morgan for his help and support and also the following artists and poets for permission to publish their work:

We would also like to thank the following artists and poets for permission to publish their work: Rosalind Atkinson, Mary Azarian, Jeanne Marie Beaumont, Nina Bogin, Jim Carruth, Catherine Flynn, Cynthia Fuller, Rebecca Gryspeerdt, Joy Harjo, John Harwood (for Gwen Harwood), Anne Hayward, Anita Klein, Miriam Magregor, Jonathan Mercer, John O'Connor, D A Prince, Joyce Sutphen, Rosemerry Wahtola Trommer.

We gratefully acknowledge permission to reprint copyright material in this book as follows:

Woman Work from *Maya Angelou: The Complete Poetry* published by Virago, copyright 2015 by The Estate of Maya Angelou, reproduced with permission of the Licensor through PLSclear; *A Rainy Sunday* by Ruby Archer from *Little Poems, in Seven Books* by Ruby Archer ©1900, by Ruby Archer, published by Braunworth, Munn and Barber, New York; *Year of the Hen* from *The Door* by Margaret Atwood published by Virago, Copyright © Margaret Atwood, 2007, reproduced with permission of the Licensor through PLSclear; *When I am in the Kitchen* by Jeanne Marie Beaumont from *Burning of the Three Fires* (BOA Editions, Ltd). Copyright 2010 by Jeanne Marie Beaumont. Reprinted by permission of the author; *Wooden Spoons* by Nina Bogin, by permission of the author; *A Ballad of Home* by Eavan Boland from *New Collected Poems* (Carcanet); *Let a Place be Made* (Vrai lieu) from *Du mouvement et de l'immobilité de Douve* by Yves Bonnefoy, © Mercure de France, 1953, translation copyright Anthony Rudolf, 2023; *Tango* from *Catch and Release* by Beverley Bie Brahic, published by The Wigtown Festival Company, winner of the 2019 Alistair Reid Pamphlet Prize, copyright 2019 Beverley Bie Brahic; *Teapot* from *White Sheets* by Beverley Bie Brahic, published by CB Editions ©Beverley Bie Brahic, 2012; *Table* by Edip Cansever was translated by Richard Tillinghast and included in *Dirty August*, Talisman House 2009, by Richard Tillinghast and Julia Clare Tillinghast; *Homecoming* from *Bale Fire* by Jim Carruth published by Polygon, an imprint of Birlinn Ltd. Copyright © Jim Carruth 2019; *Daily Bread* by Jane Clarke from *The River* (Bloodaxe Books 2015); *Being Boring* by Wendy Cope from *If I don't Know* (Faber & Faber Ltd); *This Room* by Imtiaz Dharker from *I Speak for the Devil* (Bloodaxe Books 2011); *An Expedition* by Peter Didsbury from *Scenes from a Long Sleep: New & Collected Poems* (Bloodaxe Books 2003); *Prayer* from *New Selected Poems* by Carol Ann Duffy. Published by Picador, 2004. Copyright © Carol Ann Duffy. Reproduced by permission of the author c/o Rogers, Coleridge & White Ltd., 20 Powis Mews, London W11 1JN; *Anne Hathaway* by Carol Ann Duffy from *The World's Wife* published by Picador 1999 © Carol Ann Duffy 1999; *Home* by Esme, written with First Story (firststory.org.uk) 2012; *Instructions for a Bookcase* by Catherine Flynn used by permission of the author; *Guests* by Cynthia Fuller first appeared in Background Music 2009 Flambard Press; *The Chair* by John Fuller from *Pebble & I* published by Chatto & Windus 2010 @John Fuller 2010; *Back Door* wood engraving by Bob Guy – through the Wood Engravers Society; *Perhaps the World Ends Here* from *The Woman Who Fell From The Sky* by Joy Harjo published by W W Norton & Co 1995; *Kneading Dough* wood engraving by Clifford Harper from *Timeless Simplicity* by John Lane published by Green Lane Books Ltd, Illustrations © Clifford Harper 2001-2003; *Cups* by Gwen Harwood Copyright © Estate of Gwen Harwood 2023; *Leaf-huts and Snow-houses* by Olav H Hauge, translated by Robin Fulton from *Leaf-huts and Snow-houses: Selected Poems* (Carcanet); *Scaffolding* by Seamus Heaney from *Opened Ground* (Faber & Faber Ltd); extract *A Sofa in the Forties* by Seamus Heaney from *The Spirit Level* (Faber & Faber Ltd); *Wind* by Ted Hughes from *The Hawk in the Rain* (Faber & Faber Ltd); *Table* by Robert Hull from *High Tide* published by Salt Publishing ©Robert Hull, 2010; *Winter Heart* by Jackie Kay from *Darling: New & Selected Poems* (Bloodaxe Books 2007) By permission of the publisher; *Zenith* and *A Winter Morning* by Ted Kooser from *Delights & Shadows*. Copyright ©2004 by Ted Kooser. Reprinted with the permission of The Permissions Company, LLC on behalf of Copper Canyon Press, www.coppercanyonpress.org; *Marriage* by William Letford from *Dirt* (Carcanet); *An Amish Rug* by Michael Longley from *Collected Poems* published by Jonathan Cape 2007; *The Sofa* by Jehane Markham, reproduced by permission of the author; *This Morning* by Esther Morgan from *Grace* (Bloodaxe Books 2011) and *The first warm morning* by Esther Morgan from *Beyond Calling Distance* (Bloodaxe Books 2001); *Love We're Going Home Now from 100 LOVE SONNETS: CIEN SONETOS DE AMOR* by Pablo Neruda, translated by Stephen Tapscott, Copyright © Pablo Neruda 1959 and Fundacion Pablo Neruda, Copyright © 1986 by the University of Texas Press. Courtesy of the University of Texas Press; *Teacup* and *Canals, Barges and People* by John O'Connor from *The Way of Wood Engraving* by Dorothy Braby published by London & New York, The Studio Publications 1953; *Chair* by John O'Connor from *England: An Anthology* compiled by Richard Ingrams with wood engravings by John O'Connor published by Fontana, an imprint of Harper Collins Publishers, 1991 ©Richard Ingrams 1989 and © John O'Connor 1989; *Home* by Dennis O'Driscoll from *Collected Poems* (Carcanet); *Sunlit Doorway, Sunlit Interior, Cottage Interior, Interior Manor Farm, The Workroom Window* and *Kitchen Garden Doorway* wood engravings by Howard Phipps, reproduced by permission of the artist. *The Workroom Window* was originally used as an illustration for *Steps to the River* poems by Roland Gant, Whittington Press, 1995; *Hearth, Spice Jars* and *This house* by D A Prince from *Nearly the Happy Hour* (Happenstance, 2008); *Sky Canoe* by Derryn Rees-Jones from *Quiver* published by Seren 2004; *The Slicing of Carrots* by David Scott from *Drift: New and Selected Poems* (Bloodaxe 2014); *In the Kitchen* by Penelope Shuttle © Penelope Shuttle, reproduced by kind permission of David Higham Associates; *Cat on sofa (The Picture of Dorian Grey)* by Yvonne Skargon from *The Importance of Being Oscar*, Silent Books 1988; *Home* by Mahendra Solanki from *Ten Poems about Home* (Candlestick Press, 2017) by permission of the author; *Canning* from *First Words* by Joyce Sutphen published by Red Dragonfly Press, with permission from the author; *Scandinavian Small House* by Georgia Sutton – Linocut Print Georgia Sutton @ The Big Harumph; *The Door* by Charles Tomlinson from *Swimming Chenango Lake: Selected Poems* edited by David Morley (Carcanet); *Setting* by Rosemerry Wahtola Trommer was first published in *ONE ART: An Online Journal of Poetry*; *Lattice* by Grace Wells from *the church of the love of the world* published by Dedalus Press 2022, by kind permission of www.dedaluspress.com; *Dinner with my Mother* and *Desk Duty* by Hugo Williams from *Collected Poems* (Faber & Faber Ltd); *This is Just to Say* by William Carlos Williams from *Collected Poems Vol 1 1909-1939* edited by Liz and Christopher McGowan (Carcanet); *The Kitchen Table (in memory of my mother)* by Clive Wilmer from *New and Collected Poems* (Carcanet).

Every effort has been made to trace or contact all copyright holders. The publishers would be pleased to rectify any omissions brought to their notice at the earliest opportunity.

Marriage
William Letford

I could take this opportunity
to wish you love and happiness
but you've already got that.
No, my wish for you
is the incidental, the ordinary,
to know someone
by the way their fork moves across a plate,
to see the majesty in someone's back, sleeping.
My wish for you
is twenty thousand mornings
climbing out of bed together.
My wish for you
is twenty thousand sunsets
that you can't see
because the curtains are closed and
you're sitting in a room talking about
nothing in particular.

Let the special occasions
take care of themselves,
learn to recognise
the wonder in the everyday.

My wish for you is a life lived together
filled with breakfasts, suppers, spoons and pillows.